AWESOME FAMILY NIGHTS

SUSAN LUKE

Covenant
Communications, Inc.

Dedicated with love to my parents,
Mel and Roberta Thompson.

Covenant Communications, Inc.
American Fork, Utah

Printed in the United States of America
First Printing: March 1994
94 95 96 97   10 9 8 7 6 5 4 3 2 1

Awesome Family Nights
ISBN 1–55503–689–9
Library of Congress Catalog

Covenant
Communications, Inc.

Table of Contents

Lessons

Assignment Charts

1

"The Armor of God"

"Lift up your hearts and rejoice and . . . take upon you my whole armor."
Doctrine and Covenants 27:15

OBJECT:

To help us understand how the armor of God can protect us from the fiery darts of the adversary.

PREPARATION:

1. Make two copies of the armor found on page 4. Color them, if desired, then cut them apart.
2. Using the pattern on page 5, cut out two bodies from felt cloth.
3. Gather tape and scriptures.
4. Make two "darts" following the directions given on page 3.
5. Prayerfully study Captain Moroni's preparations for war against the Lamanites found in Alma 43.
6. Assign the following scriptures: D&C 27:15-18, and 1 Peter 5:8.
7. Prepare several 2"x3" game cards by writing one question on each card that pertains to the lesson and the story of Captain Moroni. Write "Throw a fiery dart." on four or five of the blank game cards. Set the cards aside.

SUGGESTED SONG:

"I Will Be Valiant," *Children's Songbook*, page 162.

LESSON:

Display the felt figure by placing it on a flannel board or by taping it to a wall. Show your family the darts and explain that they are the "fiery darts" or temptations of the adversary. Throw them a few times at the felt figure, showing how the darts stick to the figure. Have the person assigned read 1 Peter 5:8. Satan is just waiting for any opportunity to throw his darts and destroy us. Relate the story found in Alma 43 of how Captain Moroni prepared his armies for battle against the Lamanites. Point out the fact that the Lamanite armies retreated in fear because the Nephites had better protection than they did. Also, when they were forced to do battle, the casualties were much greater on the Lamanite side because of their lack of armor. Explain to your family that just like the Nephite armies protected themselves in battle, we can do things to protect ourselves when battling the adversary. Have the person assigned read D&C 27:15-18.

After the scripture has been read, go over it again talking about each piece of armor. As each piece is mentioned, tape it to the felt figure. Discuss the meaning of each piece of armor—use the following suggestions as a guide:

Loins girt about with truth-In D&C 93:24 we learn that truth is knowledge of things as they are, and as they were, and as they are to come. Knowing the truth will help us make righteous decisions.

Breastplate of righteousness-Many of the decisions we make are guided by the feelings and emotions of our heart. If we protect our heart with a breastplate of righteousness, then the feelings and emotions that come from our heart will always be pleasing to Heavenly Father.

Feet shod with the preparation of the gospel of peace-Learning all the parts of the gospel (faith, repentance, baptism, the Holy Ghost, prayer, fasting, etc.) prepares us for battle against the adversary.

Shield of faith-Having faith in Jesus Christ and believing that he loves us and watches over us gives us peace and protection.

Helmet of salvation-Salvation is eternal life. The way we choose to live our earthly life will determine what our eternal life will be like. The helmet (which protects our head) represents salvation, and within our head is the knowledge of the gospel plan which we must follow to inherit the Celestial kingdom. We must always keep this knowledge safe in our minds if we wish to return to Heavenly Father.

Sword of my Spirit-A sword can not only defend us, but can be used as a weapon against our enemies. The Holy Ghost acts in the same way. He is there in our time of need to help us make correct decisions. He also warns us against dangers and is an invaluable weapon against the adversary.

When all the pieces are in place, have someone try to throw the darts at the figure again. Most of the darts will be repelled because of the armor. Explain that the few darts that do stick will not cause major damage because the vital parts of the body are protected. Encourage family members to always put upon them the armor of God so they can have full protection from the adversary.

GAME:

Divide into two teams. Give each team a felt figure, a dart, and one full set of armor. Use tape to attach the felt figures to a flannel board or wall. The first team draws a game card and follows the directions given. If they are to answer a question and do so correctly, they can place a piece of armor on their figure. If they answer incorrectly, they must remove a piece of armor. If they are told to throw a fiery dart at the other team and it sticks to the figure, the other team must remove a piece of armor. If the dart does not stick, the other team keeps their armor in place. Play continues back and forth until one team has all of their armor in place.

How To Make Fiery Darts

You will need:

yellow, orange, or red cellophane wrap (if not available, use regular plastic wrap)
2 tsp. popcorn seeds (or other small grain)
two rubberbands
two self-stick hook and loop (velcro) circles, 1/2"-3/4" in diameter
scissors

To assemble the darts:

1. Begin by cutting two circles from the cellophane wrap that are approximately 5" in diameter.

   Note: Only one dart is shown in the illustrations.

2. Place one teaspoon of popcorn seeds in the center of each circle.

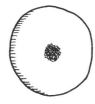

3. Bring the outside edges of the wrap together keeping the popcorn seeds in the center.

4. Place a rubber band around the cellophane just above the teaspoon of seeds.

5. If desired, cut the cellophane into strips to make it look more like fire.

6. Attach the stiff "hook" side of the hook and loop fastener to the end of the dart. Practice throwing the dart at the felt to be sure it will stick.

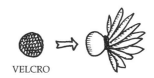

VELCRO

"Oppostion In All Things"

"For it must needs be, that there is an oppostion in all things."
2 Nephi 2:11

OBJECT:

To help family members realize the importance of opposition and adversity in our lives.

PREPARATION:

1. Copy and cut apart the word strips on pages 8 and 9 picking out the words that are most appropriate for the age levels of your family members.
2. Gather paper for paper airplanes. You may want to practice folding paper airplanes prior to the start of family home evening.
3. Prayfully study 2 Nephi 2:11-30. Be prepared to discuss these verses with your family.
4. Prayfully study D&C 122.

SUGGESTED SONG:

"Nephi's Courage," *Children's Songbook*, page 120.

LESSON:

Display the word strips randomly on the floor or on a table. Have the family members take turns finding pairs of opposites. (If your family members are young, you may need to explain the meaning of opposite.) After the activity, read 2 Nephi 2:11 and share with your family the thoughts and feelings you had as you studied 2 Nephi 2:11-30. Be sure to point out the fact that opposition was present even in the beginning (verse 15.) Explain that in order for us to have free agency, both good and evil has to exist (verse 16.) Discuss verses 22-25 to help your family understand that opposition is essential in order for Heavenly Father's plan to be fulfilled. Conclude the discussion by reading verse 27 and emphasizing the fact that we are free to choose for ourselves between good (liberty) and evil (captivity).

Opposition can also make us stronger. Relate the story of Joseph Smith found in D&C 122. Explain that according to the Lord, every trial he endured was for his own good and gave him experience. God was always with him and will remain with him forever. The trials we face in our lives may be different than Joseph Smith's, but they are for our own good and give us experience. Our trials make us stronger.

6

OBJECT LESSON:

To demonstrate how our trials can actually make us stronger, hold up a flat piece of paper and try to make it "fly" through the air. Point out how poorly the paper flies. Now begin folding and creasing the paper into an airplane. Explain as you fold the paper that each crease represents a trial (mentioning possible trials as you fold.) With each fold (trial) the paper becomes stronger until eventually it can fly through the air gracefully. Our lives are very similar. Just like the folds make the paper stronger, trials make us stronger. Some of our trials may seem hard at the time but Heavenly Father is always mindful of us. Each trial that we endure brings greater strength and experience into our lives.

ACTIVITY:

Pass out paper to everyone and have fun making paper airplanes. Have a contest to see whose plane flies the farthest, fastest, highest, etc. In preparation for this activity, you may want to check your local library for books on paper airplanes.

Handy Hint #1

Try having family home evening in the car. One year we had a patriotic lesson in the car while we were driving to a distant park to set off fireworks. It was a great way to keep everyone stationary during the lesson (which is an impossible task at our house!)

GOOD	BAD
BLACK	WHITE
HAPPY	SAD
LIGHT	DARK
DAY	NIGHT
BEGINNING	END
UP	DOWN
MAN	WOMAN
CREATE	DESTROY
GIVE	TAKE

RIGHTEOUSNESS	WICKEDNESS
BIG	LITTLE
TEMPORAL	ETERNAL
SORROW	JOY
TRUE	FALSE
FATHER	MOTHER
BROTHER	SISTER
FREEDOM	CAPTIVITY
ON	OFF
STOP	GO

"Family Responsibilities"

"All things work together for good to them that love God."
Romans 8:28

OBJECT:

To help family members realize that we must all share in the responsibilities of the family.

PREPARATION:

1. Copy and color the house picture on page 12. Cut the picture into several puzzle pieces so that each person has at least one or two pieces. Write one family chore or responsibility on the back of each puzzle piece.
2. If you have young children, you may want to make them each a set of chore tags. To do so, follow the directions given on page 13.
3. Gather several large rocks, a felt pen, a bucket, and one paper sack for each family member. Using a permanent marker, label each rock with a different family chore or responsibility.

SUGGESTED SONG:

"When We're Helping," *Children's Songbook*, page 198.

LESSON:

Give everyone a piece or pieces of the puzzle. Tell them that each puzzle piece represents a family responsibility and that various responsibilities are written on the back of each piece. Have one person try to put the puzzle together by using only their piece or pieces of the puzzle. Explain that even though one person might fulfill their responsibilities the house will not be in order unless others help. Have another family member add their piece or pieces. Explain that even though two members may have fulfilled their responsibilities the house is still not in order. Continue until everyone has had a chance to add their pieces to the puzzle. Explain that everyone needs to work together and fulfill their responsibilities for the house to be in order. It is important that everyone does their share so that one person does not feel over-burdened. Demonstrate this by placing the bucket on the floor or on a table and setting the previously prepared rocks around the bucket. Place the rocks into the bucket one at a time mentioning the chore listed on each rock. When all of the rocks are in the bucket, have everyone take a turn lifting the bucket. Ask if they would like

10

the responsibility of carrying the bucket full of rocks all day long. Of course not! Ask the family members if they would all be willing to share the responsibilities. After they have answered, pass out a sack to each member of the family. Distribute the rocks (chores) evenly having the family members place their rocks into their sack. When all the rocks have been distributed, have the family members lift their sacks and decide which one was easier to carry, the sack or the bucket. Explain that it's easier for everyone to carry their own share of the responsibilities that it is for one person to carry them all.

ACTIVITY:

As a family, work out a schedule of responsibilities so that everyone can do their share of the work. Our family has used the the following method successfully for quite some time (see sample below). The names of our four older children are listed in order from one to four on each day of the calender (rotating the order each day). The child in the number one position is in charge of the living room, diapers, helping with dinner, and unloading the dishwasher. The number two child is in charge of the kitchen, dressing (the little boys), clearing the table, and scraping the dishes. The number three child is in charge of the bathroom, feeding (the little boys), setting the table, and loading the dishwasher. The number four child has the day off (occasionally helping their younger sister with her jobs). Everyone is responsible for keeping their bedrooms clean and picking up after themselves. We also refer to this chart as the "Harmony Chart." (Personally, I like to think of it as Mom and Dad's "Sanity Chart!") When disagreements (or more appropriately, battles!) arise over who gets to sit in the front seat of the car, or the favorite chair in the family room, or who gets the biggest cookie, etc., it's easy to say the number one person has the privilege for the day.

"Harmony Chart"
May 1994

1. Living room, diapers, dinner, unloading
2. Kitchen, dressing, clearing, scraping
3. Bathroom, feeding, setting table, loading
4. Day off

Sunday	Monday	Tuesday	Wednesday	Thursday	Friday	Saturday
1 Chris Kim Corinne Karalyn	2 Karalyn Chris Kim Corinne	3 Corinne Karalyn Chris Kim	4 Kim Corinne Karalyn Chris	5 Chris Kim Corinne Karalyn	6 Karalyn Chris Kim Corinne	7 Corinne Karalyn Chris Kim
8	9	10	11	12	13	14

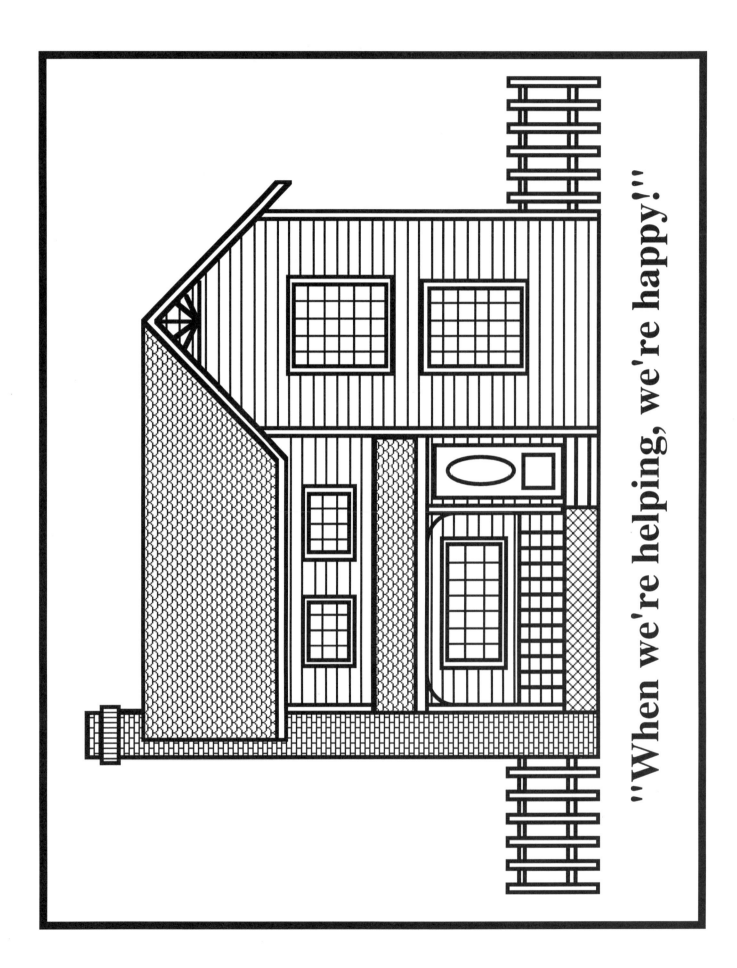

"When we're helping, we're happy!"

Chore Tags

After making copies of these chore tags, color, cut, laminate, and punch holes where indicated. Gather six small cup hooks and screw them into a small board. Attach a picture hanger to the back of the board. Hang one tag on each hook and display the board within easy reach of your child. After your child completes one of the chores, have him or her turn the tag over and hang it back on the cup hook. If you draw a smiling face or place a fun sticker on the back of each tag before you laminate it, turning over the tag will be even more fun.

MAKE YOUR BED

GET DRESSED

BRUSH YOUR TEETH

COMB YOUR HAIR

PICK UP YOUR TOYS

SAY YOUR PRAYERS

4

"The Holy Ghost"

"And by the power of the Holy Ghost ye may know the truth of all things."
Moroni 10:5

OBJECT:

To help family members appreciate the importance of the Holy Ghost as a guide in our lives.

PREPARATION:

1. Make a copy of pages 16 and 17.
2. Gather four coins of four different denominations (quarter, dime, nickel, penny.)
3. Using the page with the blank circles, randomly write in one of the coin amounts in four of the circles, then another four circles with another coin amount, and so on until all the circles have been used.
4. Gather a flashlight, a watch with a second hand, and a rolled up newspaper.

SUGGESTED SONG:

"The Still Small Voice," *Children's Songbook*, page 106.

LESSON/ACTIVITY:

Place the paper that has the circles with the shapes on a table. Explain to your family that the influence of the Holy Ghost is a gift from Heavenly Father to help guide and direct our lives. The activity that they are about to watch (or participate in) will help teach them what their life would be like without the influence of the Holy Ghost. Ask a family member to come forward and place each coin in a circle. (Secretly decide ahead of time which type of coin will belong to which shape. For instance, the four largest coins could be placed on the four circles with the triangles, the next largest coins on the circles with the squares, etc.) Do not give any instructions; let them figure out the system by themselves. Every time they place a coin on the wrong circle, tap them on the head with the newspaper roll. Don't tap them if they place a coin correctly. Continue this process until eventually they figure out that a certain size of coin belongs to a certain kind of circle. When finished, explain that without instructions (or guidance) we can only learn by trial and error.

Sometimes we get "tapped on the head" several times before we learn. If we live in tune with the Holy Ghost, we can eliminate the guess work and always make right choices.

Now explain to your family that the next activity will teach them how the Holy Ghost helps them in their lives. Place the other paper (the one with the handwritten coin amounts) on the table. Using a watch with a secondhand, time each family member as they take a turn placing each coin in its appropriate circle. Record the times. When finished, explain that the information in each circle helped to guide us in correctly placing each coin. The Holy Ghost guides us in our lives. When we listen to him, we can make correct choices.

Next, determine which time was the slowest and challenge the person with the fastest time to play again, beating the slowest time. They're going to think it's a breeze! As they begin, turn off all the lights in the room so that they can no longer see to place the coins correctly. Explain that if we don't listen to the Holy Ghost, or are unworthy to receive his help, it's just like playing the game in the dark with nothing to guide us. Now turn on the flashlight, covering most of the lens with your hand. Explain that Christ is the light in the darkness and he has sent the Holy Ghost to "enlighten our minds" (D&C 11:13). As we obey the commandments, the Holy Ghost shines brighter in our lives. Ask family members to take turns naming things they can do to bring the guidance of the Holy Ghost into their lives (church attendance, scripture study, paying tithes, fasting, etc.) With each thing mentioned, let a little more light shine through. During the discussion, encourage the person that was challenged to continue to place the coins on the correct circles. Keep the discussion going until all of the lights in the room can once again be turned on. Point out that without the lights it was extremely difficult for the family member to place all the coins correctly. This is similar to what our lives would be like without the influence of the Holy Ghost; it would be extremely difficult to make correct decisions.

Conclude by bearing your testimony and challenging family members to live their lives worthy of receiving guidance and direction from the Holy Ghost.

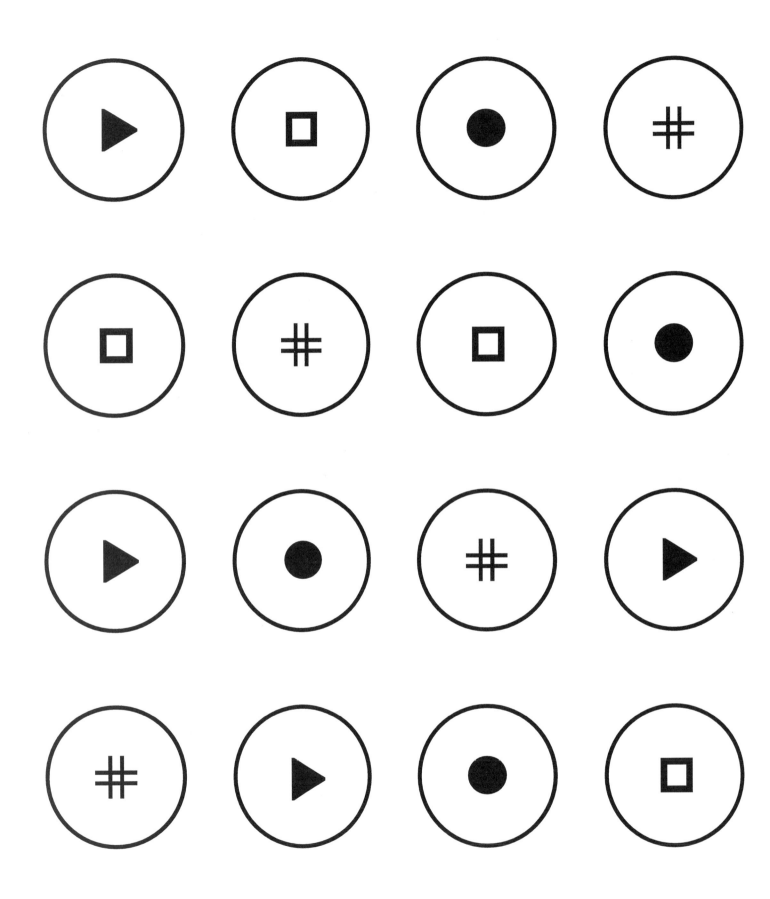

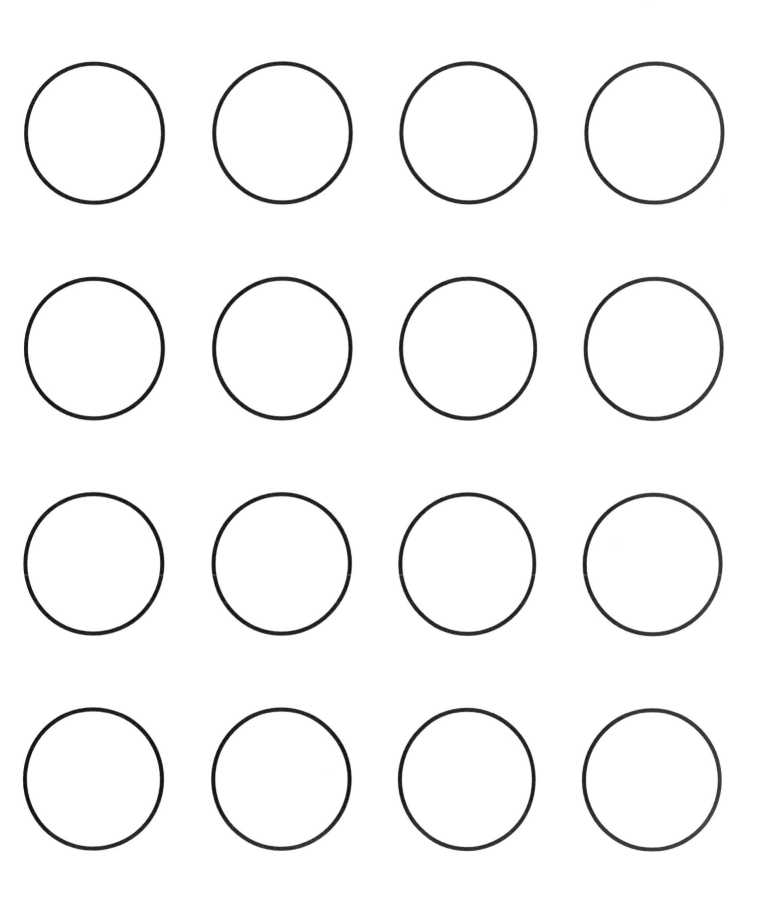

"Building Self-Esteem"

"Remember the worth of souls is great in the sight of God."
Doctrine and Covenants 18:10

OBJECT:

To help build each other's self-esteem by treating each other with love, kindness and respect.

PREPARATION:

1. Copy, color, cut, and laminate (if desired) the "THANKS" banner and several stars.
2. Prepare play dough by using the following recipe:

   <u>PLAY DOUGH</u>

1 cup flour	1 cup water
1/2 cup salt	1 Tbs. cooking oil
2 tsp. cream of tarter	3-4 drops food coloring

   In a sauce pan, mix together dry ingredients. Add liquids and cook for 3 minutes over medium heat, stirring constantly. (Dough will thicken like mashed potatoes.) Remove from heat and knead immediately. Store in airtight container.

3. Write a short spotlight on each family member to be read during Family Home Evening. Include several positive comments in each spotlight.
4. Gather a bean bag or small ball.

SUGGESTED SONG:

"Kindness Begins with Me," *Children's Songbook*, page 145.

LESSON:

Begin by showing the clay to your family and rolling it into a cylinder shape that is about 2" in diameter and 5" tall. Place it upright onto a flat surface so that it looks like a tree trunk. Tell your family that the clay represents a person. Explain to the family that unfortunately the average person will receive far more negative comments in their lifetime than positive comments. Some experts say as many as 100,000 negative comments in the first 20 years! Ask your family what some of these negative comments might be. As each comment is mentioned, remove a chunk of clay from the base of the "trunk." Continue removing chunks of clay until the trunk falls over. Point out to your family how negative comments can weaken and destroy us. Now do the opposite and have the family members mention positive comments as you add the clay back to the weakened spot. Continue until all of the clay that was removed is returned to the base. (Extra clay could be added around the base to make it even stronger than before.) Explain to your family that positive comments help to build a person and strengthen them.

In Psalms 82:6, we learn that we are all "children of the most High." Heavenly Father created each one of us and we are all important. We should always treat each other kindly and build each other by offering sincere compliments and having respect for each other.

ACTIVITY:

Pass out a piece of paper and pencil to each family member. Have them write their first name vertically down the left side of the paper using large letters. Now have them pass their paper to the person on their left. When each family member receives a paper, have them write something nice about the person whose name is listed on the paper using one of the letters as the first letter of their compliment. When finished, pass the paper again to the left. Continue until everyone has had a chance to add a comment to each paper. (Note: If someone has a short name and is in a large family, more than one comment could be added to each letter. If someone has a long name and is in a small family, each person could write comments for two or more letters.) Take turns reading the comments written about each person.

GAME:

Have the family members sit in a circle. Start by having someone toss the bean bag or ball to another family member. The person that caught the bean bag or ball then says something nice about the person that tossed it. The play continues in the same manner until everyone has had plenty of opportunities to toss, catch, and compliment.

CONCLUSION:

To help promote kindness throughout the week and to encourage family members to look for the positive characteristics of others, display the "THANKS" banner in a visible place in your home. Encourage family members to look for other family members who are showing kindness, love, and respect for others. When something is noticed, write the name of the family member and what was noticed on a star and display it by the banner. See how many stars your family can display before the next family home evening.

6

"Seeking Christ"

". . . those that seek me early shall find me."
Proverbs 8:17

OBJECT:

To learn what we must do to find Christ in our lives.

PREPARATION:

1. Prepare the clue cards by following the directions given on page 23.
2. Place a picture of Christ where the final clue leads (preferably by a bright lamp).

SUGGESTED SONG:

"Seek the Lord Early," *Children's Songbook*, page 108.

LESSON:

This is a fun activity of reading scriptures to help us learn what we must do to find Christ in our lives. It also allows us to look up other scriptures as clues that will help lead us in our search for Christ. At each stop, spend time discussing the topic and scripture mentioned on the clue card. Continue the search by reading the scripture listed on the card that contains the next clue. After all the clues have been read and the picture of Christ has been found, close by sharing your testimony of Christ.

Copy the cards on this page and on the following page. Cut them apart. Set card #1 aside for your family to use in beginning their search for Christ. Place the remaining cards around the house as follows:

Place card #2 in a cup.
Place card #3 on a pillow.
Place card #4 by a salt shaker.
Place card #5 in the oven.
Place card #6 by something musical (piano, stereo, instrument, etc.).
Place card #7 by a furnace or heater.
Place card #8 by an iron.

Place card #9 by a sewing machine or needlework.
Place card #10 in a closet.
Place card #11 by a water faucet.
Place card #12 by a window.
Place card #13 by soap or detergent.
Place card #14 with a picture of Christ by a bright lamp.

1

We must diligently seek for Christ.
(1 Nephi 10:19)

For your next clue, read:
Matthew 26:27

2

We must pray always to find Christ.
(D&C 19:38)

For your next clue, read:
2 Nephi 33:3

3

Fasting will bring us closer
to Christ.
(Alma 5:46)

For your next clue, read:
Matthew 5:13

4

We can find Christ through
service to others.
(Mosiah 2:17)

For your next clue, read:
Hosea 7:6

5

We can find Christ through scripture
study.
(John 5:39)

For your next clue, read:
D&C 136:28

6

Paying tithes and fast offerings will
help us to find Christ.
(D&C 119:4)

For your next clue, read:
4 Nephi 1:32

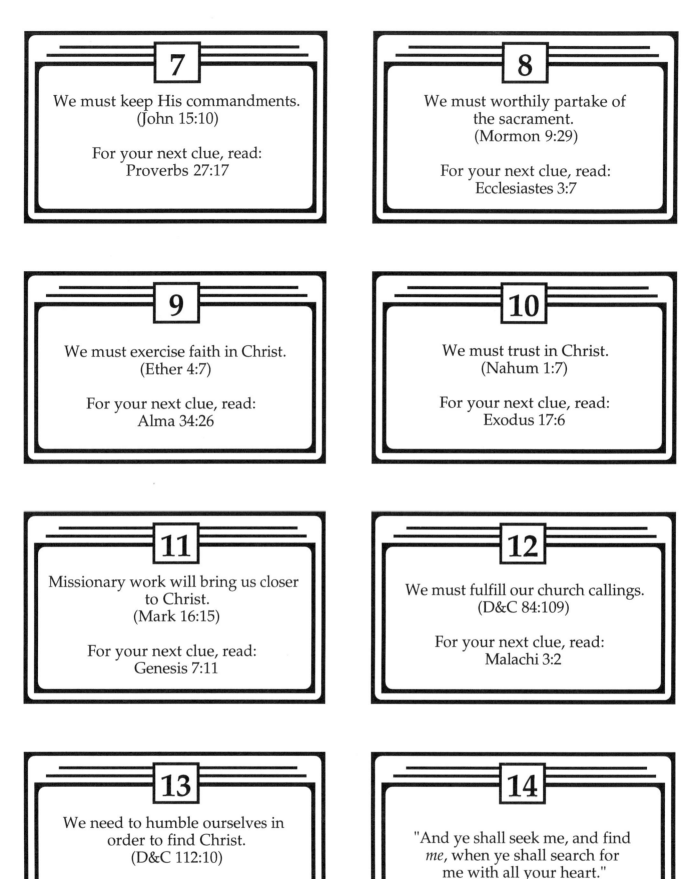

7

We must keep His commandments.
(John 15:10)

For your next clue, read:
Proverbs 27:17

8

We must worthily partake of
the sacrament.
(Mormon 9:29)

For your next clue, read:
Ecclesiastes 3:7

9

We must exercise faith in Christ.
(Ether 4:7)

For your next clue, read:
Alma 34:26

10

We must trust in Christ.
(Nahum 1:7)

For your next clue, read:
Exodus 17:6

11

Missionary work will bring us closer
to Christ.
(Mark 16:15)

For your next clue, read:
Genesis 7:11

12

We must fulfill our church callings.
(D&C 84:109)

For your next clue, read:
Malachi 3:2

13

We need to humble ourselves in
order to find Christ.
(D&C 112:10)

For your next clue, read:
D&C 33:17

14

"And ye shall seek me, and find
me, when ye shall search for
me with all your heart."
Jeremiah 29:13

24

7

"Put a Smile On Your Face"

"Let us cheerfully do all things that lie in our power."
Doctrine & Covenants 123:17

OBJECT:

To help family members realize how good and bad feelings in the home affect everyone.

PREPARATION:

1. Prepare visual aids following the instructions given on page 27.
2. Make a copy of the Evaluation Sheet on page 30 for each family member.
3. Gather pens or pencils.

SUGGESTED SONG:

"If you Chance to Meet a Frown," *Children's Songbook*, page 78.

LESSON:

Sometimes when we argue and disagree, we feel there is really no harm in it. We might think that it only affects those who are arguing. To show the family that this is not so, demonstrate the following:

Hold up the cardboard labeled "BAD FEELINGS." Ask family members what kind of bad feelings they have noticed at times in the family. As they mention them, place a string with a "bad face" attached to it in one of the slits. Continue this until all of the "bad faces" are hanging down from the cardboard. Now explain to the family that these faces represent the bad feelings that can exist in our home. It's almost as if they float through the air. Hold the cardboard up and ask a family member to walk straight through the strings without ducking or swerving from side to side. After they've walked through, ask if any of the bad feelings hit them in the face. Of course they did. Explain that everything we do in our family affects each other. You may want to allow time for family members to talk about how they are affected individually by these bad feelings.

Now hold up the cardboard labeled "GOOD FEELINGS." Have the family members name things that create good feelings in the home. As they are mentioned, hang a happy face in each slit. When all of the happy faces are in place, have the family members walk through them the same as they did with the bad feelings and see if they get hit in the face by the happy feelings. Explain that no matter what feelings we have, good or bad, they "float" through the air and affect every member of the family. You may want to talk about how some of the family members have been affected by good feelings in the home.

DEMONSTRATION:

To demonstrate how our actions can have an affect on the rest of the family, show them the bowl of water. Be sure the water is perfectly calm and explain that a family is like a calm body of water. When we drop a rock or something into the bowl of water, how does it affect it? Was any of the water able to stay calm and unaffected? This is the same in our family. When anyone does something, good or bad, the ripples go out and affect everyone. You can demonstrate the same thing by using a glass of water and food coloring. When a drop of food coloring (good or bad feelings) is dropped into the water (the family) the whole amount (after stirring) is affected.

ACTIVITY:

Have everyone fill out an Evaluation Sheet, helping the younger ones as needed. When finished, have family members tally up their scores and see how they rated. Family members don't have to reveal their scores if they don't want to. If some family members didn't score very well, you may want to talk to them individually and help them create a plan to promote more happiness in the home.

To encourage happiness throughout the week, assign each family member to be in charge of another family member's happiness for the whole week. If successful, reassign at the following Family Home Evening. To make it even more interesting, you could keep the assignments secret and then try to guess at the next Family Home Evening who was in charge of who. By doing it this way, it will encourage family members to be nice to everyone, so that they won't give themselves away during the week.

When finished, remove the string from the happy faces and tape them around the house to remind the family of their responsibility to promote happiness.

BAD FEELINGS

GOOD FEELINGS

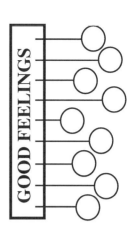

GOOD FEELINGS

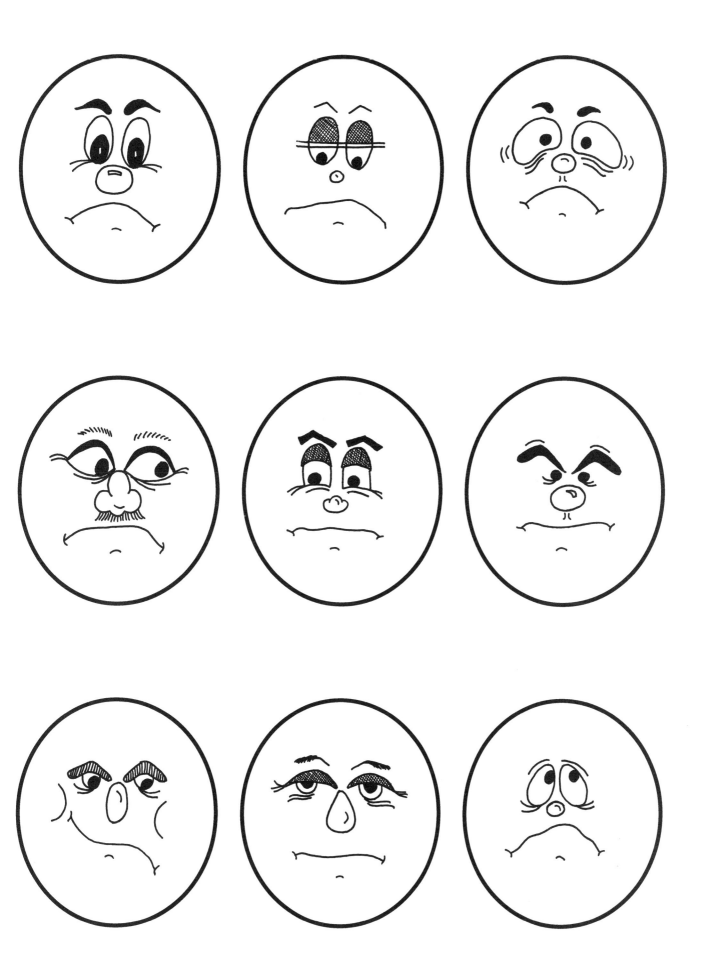

EVALUATION SHEET

	Most of the Time	Some of the Time	Needs a Little Work
1. Do I try hard to get along with every member of my family?	☐	☐	☐
2. When asked to do something, do I do it with a smile?	☐	☐	☐
3. Do I help others whenever I have the opportunity?	☐	☐	☐
4. Do I think of other family members before myself?	☐	☐	☐
5. Do I share what I have with others in the family?	☐	☐	☐
6. Do I do my share of the work around the house?	☐	☐	☐
7. Do I try hard to make other family members happy?	☐	☐	☐
8. Do I avoid arguing with other family members?	☐	☐	☐
9. Do I do nice things around the house without being asked?	☐	☐	☐
10. Do I try to look for the good in every situation?	☐	☐	☐

TOTALS ☐ + ☐ + ☐ = ☐

Score 3 points for every "Most of the Time" answer, 2 points for every "Some of the Time" answer, and 1 point for every "Needs a Little Work" answer. If your total points are between 23 and 30, you are doing a good job at bringing happiness into your home. If your total points are between 15 and 22, you are doing pretty good, but could try a little harder in some areas. If your points total between 1 and 14, you need to work harder at bringing happiness into your home!

8

"Family Night at the Movies"

"But behold, they did watch steadfastly."
3 Nephi 1:8

OBJECT:

To have fun together as a family viewing an uplifting movie.

PREPARATION:

1. Copy the marquee and write the movie title on the lines provided.
2. Copy a movie ticket and snack coupons for each member of the family. Optional: You can perforate the snack coupons by removing the thread from your sewing machine and stitching in between the coupons.
3. Gather snacks and copy enough snack labels for each member of the family. Color and cut the labels and attach them to the appropriate snacks by following the directions on page 34.
4. Set up the family room like a movie theater and the kitchen like a snack bar.

SUGGESTED SONG:

"The Family," *Children's Songbook*, page 194.

ACTIVITY:

This is a fun family home evening so when planning it, you may want to consider inviting other family or friends to share in the activities (and preparations)! If desired, turn your family room into a movie theater by setting up rows of chairs and placing the marquee on the outside door of the "theater" advertising the movie. Set up the kitchen like a snack bar. Hand out the movie tickets and snack coupons to everyone. Let one family member work the snack bar, another take movie tickets, and another be an usher and show people to their seats. (You may even want to turn down the lights and let the usher use a flashlight). When everyone is ready, start the movie and enjoy!

NOW PLAYING!

33

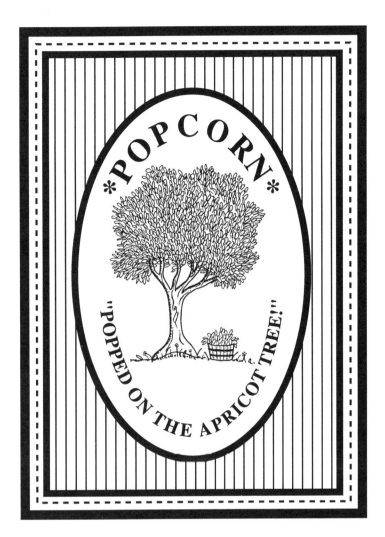

POPCORN

"POPPED ON THE APRICOT TREE!"

How To Use The Labels-

After coloring and cutting the labels, glue the popcorn label to the front of a brown paper lunch sack. Fill the sack with popcorn.

Wrap store bought or homemade cookies with plastic wrap. Secure the plastic wrap with tape. Glue the label to the front of the wrapped cookie, or place the label on the front of the wrapped cookie and place another layer of plastic wrap around the entire cookie, securing the label in the process. Secure the plastic wrap with tape.

Glue the punch label to the front of a paper cup or a can of pop.

HEAVENLY COOKIES

"For a taste that's out of this world!"

PARADISE PUNCH

One sip and you'll be in a "state of happiness!"

34

9

"The True Church"

"For thus shall my church be called in the last days, even
The Church of Jesus Christ of Latter-day Saints."
Doctrine and Covenants 115:4

OBJECT:

To help family members understand that we, as Latter-day Saints, belong to the true church of Jesus Christ.

PREPARATION:

1. Make three copies of page 39. Color, then cut the pieces apart.
2. Gather three envelopes. Label the first two envelopes: Church A and Church B. Place a partial set of church pieces in each of these two envelopes, making each set slightly different. Place a full set of church pieces in the third envelope and label it "The Church of Jesus Christ of Latter-day Saints." (Note: When organizing the partial sets for the first two envelopes, be sure to omit pieces that are exclusive to the only true church, i.e., proper priesthood authority, saving ordinances, will bear the name of Christ, modern-day revelation, etc.).

SUGGESTED SONG:

"The Church of Jesus Christ," *Children's Songbook*, page 77.

LESSON:

Lay envelopes A and B on a table or floor for your family to see. Explain that tonight they are going to help organize the true church. Starting with envelope A, have a family member pull one piece out at a time and read what is written. Look up the scripture reference and read it aloud. Discuss the scripture and then put the puzzle piece in place. (Refer to the illustration on page 38 for the proper placement of the puzzle pieces.) Continue until all of the pieces in the envelope have been used. Point out to the family that although this church has many good qualities, it is not complete and is not the true church of Jesus Christ. Continue this same process with the next envelope, looking up any new scripture references. When finished, look over the partially completed churches and explain to your family that none of them could be the true church because they are lacking essential pieces to the puzzle. Show them the final envelope. Have them take turns choosing a puzzle piece, looking up the scripture reference (if it is a new reference), and putting the puzzle piece in its proper place. When the puzzle is complete, review all the pieces of the true church and point out that The Church of Jesus Christ of Latter-day Saints is the only church on the earth today that has the fully restored gospel of Jesus Christ.

GAME:

Designate one family member to be in charge of randomly reading the game questions below. Divide the rest of the family into two teams. Give each team a complete set of puzzle pieces. Each team takes turns answering questions. When a question is answered correctly, put a puzzle piece in place. If an incorrect answer is given, no piece is earned and play proceeds with the other team. Continue until each team has built their church.

Game Questions

1. What day was the church of Jesus Christ organized and established in these latter-days? (April 6, 1830, D&C 21:3)
2. What is the name of the true church of Christ? (The Church of Jesus Christ of Latter-day Saints, D&C 115:4)
3. Name three saving ordinances performed in the temple. (sealings, baptisms for the dead, endowments)
4. Who is the head of the church? (Christ, Ephesians 5:23)
5. How is the Holy Ghost received? (by the laying on of hands, D&C 35:6)
6. What is the proper way to baptize? (by immersion by one having proper priesthood authority, D&C 20:73-74)
7. At what age are children to be baptized? (eight years old, D&C 68:27)
8. How much of our income is paid as tithing to the Lord? (one-tenth, D&C 119:4)
9. Name three ordained offices within the Aaronic Priesthood. (deacon, teacher, priest, D&C 107:10)
10. Name three ordained offices within the Melchizedek Priesthood. (elder, seventy, high priest, patriarch, and apostle; Bible dictionary—see "Melchizedek Priesthood")
11. How many apostles did Christ have during his time on earth, during the time of the Nephites, and currently? (twelve, Luke 6:13, 3 Nephi 12:1)
12. Who wrote the Articles of Faith? (Joseph Smith, The Articles of Faith)
13. Name four auxiliaries in the Church. (Relief Society, Sunday School, Primary, Young Men, Young Women)
14. Who presides over a ward? (a bishop, D&C 107:73-74)
15. Name the two prominent civilizations mentioned in the Book of Mormon. (Nephites and Lamanites)
16. Name the two Priesthoods. (Aaronic and Melchizedek, D&C 107:6)
17. Name the three kingdoms of glory. (Telestial, Terrestrial, Celestial, D&C 76: 91-92)

18. Who conferred the Melchizedek Priesthood upon Joseph Smith and Oliver Cowdery? (Peter, James, and John, D&C 27:12)
19. Who receives and announces revelations for the Church? (the prophet, D&C 28:2-8)
20. What did Joseph Smith use to translate the plates of gold? (Urim and Thummim, Joseph Smith—History 1:35)
21. Did the true church exist among the Nephites and Lamanites? (yes, Helaman 11:21)
22. How do you become a member of the true church? (through baptism, after having a broken heart and contrite spirit and having repented of all sins, Moroni 6:2)
23. Who told Joseph Smith about the gold plates? (the angel Moroni, Joseph Smith—History 1:33-34)
24. How old was Joseph Smith when he received his first vision? (fourteen, Joseph Smith—History 1:7)
25. Who ordained Joseph Smith and Oliver Cowdery to the Aaronic Priesthood? (John the Baptist, Joseph Smith—History 1:72)
26. What book of scriptures is filled with latter-day instructions from God? (Doctrine and Covenants)
27. What is an endowment? (a spiritual gift from Heavenly Father, D&C 105:11-12)
28. What does it mean to be sealed to your family? (to be bound to them eternally, D&C 132:46)
29. Why do we perform baptisms for the dead? (so that our unbaptized ancestors will have the chance to enter the Kingdom of God, D&C 138:32-34)
30. Why do we need to be baptized? (so we can enter the Kingdom of God, John 3:5)
31. Who are the three members of the Godhead? (God the Father, Jesus Christ, and the Holy Ghost, Articles of Faith 1:1)
32. Where was the first temple of this dispensation built? (Kirtland, Ohio, D&C 109:2)
33. By what power was the earth and heavens created? (by the power of the Melchizedek Priesthood, Jeremiah 51:15)
34. Name three spiritual gifts. (healing, speaking in tongues, discernment, interpretation of tongues, revelation, working miracles, etc.)
35. What is a miracle? (a wonderous act of God)
36. Why do people serve missions? (to proclaim the gospel of Jesus Christ, D&C 66:5)
37. Were the early Saints persecuted for their beliefs? (yes, D&C 99:1)
38. Why do we partake of the Sacrament? (to remember Jesus and to renew the covenants we made at baptism, D&C 20:77,79)
39. Which two sets of scriptures contain the sacrament prayers: the Bible, the Book of Mormon, the Doctrine and Covenants or the Pearl of Great Price? (Book of Mormon, Moroni 4 & 5, and Doctrine and Covenants, D&C 20:77,79)
40. Is the church of Jesus Christ also known as the kingdom of God? (yes, D&C 138:44)
41. Which day of the week is set aside to worship Heavenly Father? (Sunday)

42. Were there temples built in ancient times? (yes, Bible Dictionary—see "Temple")
43. What is another name for believing in something that you can't see, but is true? (faith, Alma 32:21)
44. What did Joseph Smith do in order to find out which church was true? (he prayed and asked Heavenly Father, Joseph Smith—History 1:13-14)
45. What two heavenly personages appeared to Joseph Smith in the sacred grove? (Heavenly Father and Jesus Christ, Joseph Smith—History 1:17)
46. Who is the chief cornerstone of the Church? (Jesus Christ, Ephesians 2:20)
47. During Christ's time, were the members of the church called saints? (yes, Romans 1:7)
48. What is a seer? (a revelator and a prophet, Mosiah 8:15-18)
49. Did Joseph Smith translate all of the plates that Moroni gave to him? (no, part of the plates were sealed, Joseph Smith—History 1:65)
50. How old was Joseph Smith when the angel Moroni appeared to him for the first time? (seventeen, Joseph Smith—History 1:28-33)

Note: The following illustration shows the proper placement of the puzzle pieces.

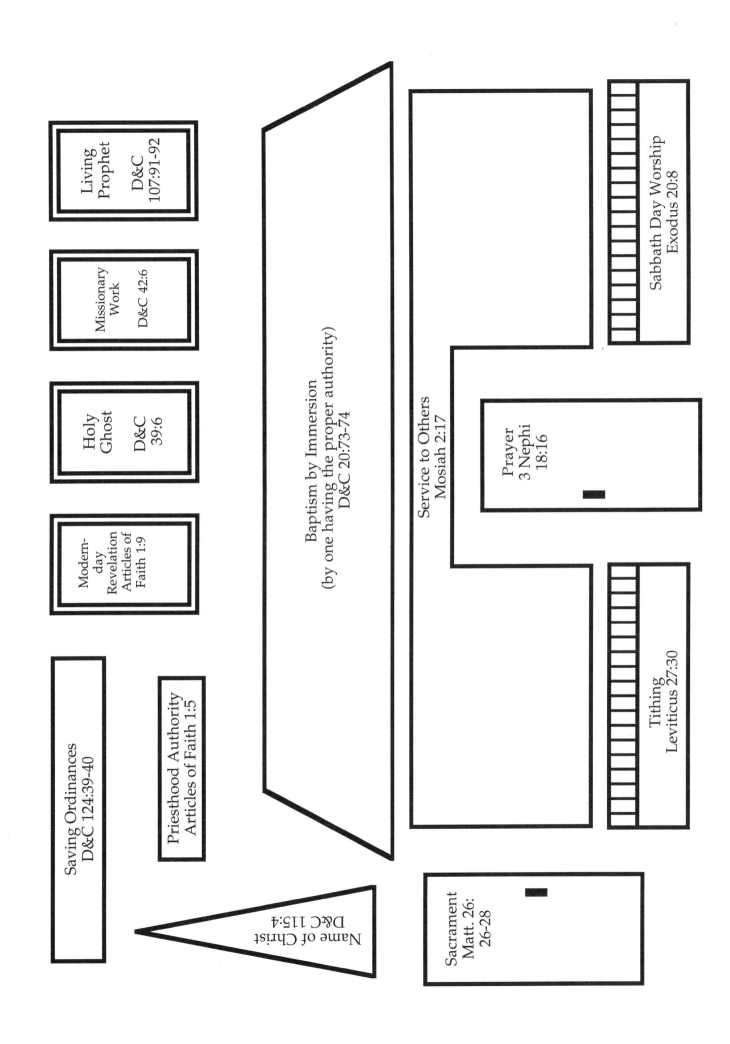

Living Prophet
D&C 107:91-92

Missionary Work
D&C 42:6

Holy Ghost
D&C 39:6

Modern-day Revelation
Articles of Faith 1:9

Saving Ordinances
D&C 124:39-40

Priesthood Authority
Articles of Faith 1:5

Baptism by Immersion
(by one having the proper authority)
D&C 20:73-74

Name of Christ
D&C 115:4

Service to Others
Mosiah 2:17

Sabbath Day Worship
Exodus 20:8

Prayer
3 Nephi 18:16

Tithing
Leviticus 27:30

Sacrament
Matt. 26: 26-28

"Obedience to Laws and Rules"

"Hearken and hear and obey the law which I shall give unto you."
Doctrine & Covenants 42:2

OBJECT:

To help family members realize that laws and rules are to help us, not hinder us.

PREPARATION:

1. Copy the game board and game cards on pages 42, 43, and 44 (enlarging game board if desired). Cut the game cards apart. Color the game board (optional).
2. Gather a different playing piece (button, coin, etc.) for each family member to use during the game.
3. Gather a shallow plate, a large bowl with high sides, a marble, and a coin.

SUGGESTED SONG:

"Quickly I'll Obey," *Children's Songbook*, page 197.

LESSON:

Have one family member stand and hold onto the edges of the plate. Place the marble on the plate and ask them to tilt the plate back and forth in a circular motion so that the marble rolls around the plate. Have them make the marble roll as fast as possible without falling off. Let other family members try if they desire. Explain to the family that even though this can be done, the marble needs to roll slowly to prevent it from falling off the plate. Now have the family members take turns holding the bowl and rolling the marble around in the same way. See how fast the marble can roll around in the bowl without falling out. Point out that the high sides of the bowl allow the marble to reach greater speeds. Explain that this is an example of how our life is affected by laws and rules. The plate represents what our lives would be like without laws and rules. We may think that without laws and rules we would have more freedom, but this is untrue. The sides of the plate are low, giving the appearance of freedom, but actually confine the plate to only slight movements to keep the marble from falling off. The bowl with the high sides represents our lives with laws and rules. The high sides of the bowl may look confining, but they actually allow the marble to roll around easily, uniformly, and at much higher speeds than the plate allows. When we have laws and rules to guide us, we actually have more freedom to fulfill our potential.

Discuss with your family the different laws and rules they follow by using the suggested topics and questions listed below. Be sure to emphasize the fact that by following rules we achieve more freedom.

LAWS OF THE LAND-

What are some of these laws? Discuss different laws of the land.

Why should we obey them? We are commanded to obey the laws of the land (The Articles of Faith 1:12, D&C 58:21-22, and D&C 98:4-6).

What would happen if we should break them? Just as in the days of King Mosiah, we are left to the punishments established by the laws of the land (Mosiah:29:15).

LAWS OF HEAVENLY FATHER-

What are some of these laws? The Ten Commandments (Exodus 20:3-17).

Why should we keep them? The Lord's laws are perfect (Psalms 19:7). They bring freedom (D&C 98:8), happiness (Proverbs 29:18), and peace (Psalms 119:165).

What would happen if we should break them? We would inherit a lesser kingdom (D&C 88:21-24).

LAWS OF THE FAMILY-

What are some of these laws? Discuss your family's rules.

Why should we keep them? We are commanded to establish a house of order (D&C 88:119.) As children, we are to obey our parents in all things (Col. 3:20).

What would happen if we should break them? Discuss various consequences for breaking family rules.

After discussing family rules, you may want to write them down and post them where all family members can see them throughout the coming weeks.

GAME:

To play the game "RULES OF THE HOUSE," place the game cards face down in the space indicated on the game board. Place the previously gathered playing pieces at the start. At each turn, determine the amount of spaces you will move by flipping a coin, moving one space for "heads" and two spaces for "tails." Or, place a small piece of tape on each side of the coin and label one side "1" and the other side "2." If you land on a space labeled "Draw one card," follow the written directions then return the card face down at the bottom of the pile. Play continues until everyone reaches the finish.

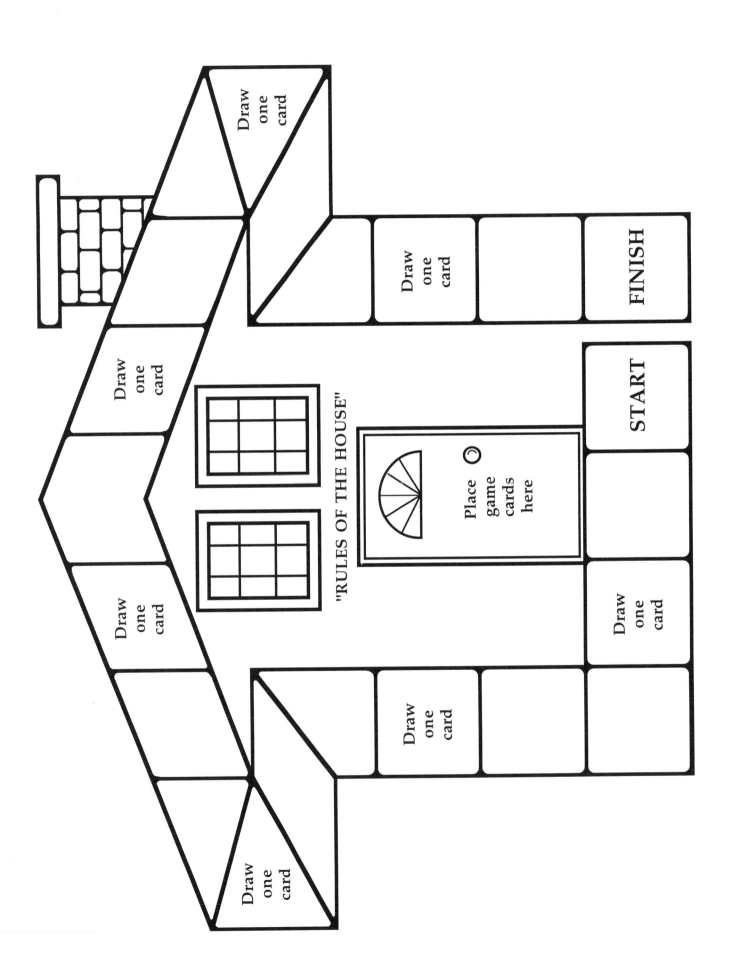

You came home from your friend's house on time!

Move ahead two spaces!

You completed your homework before dinner!

Move ahead two spaces!

You put your game away when you were done playing!

Move ahead two spaces!

You brushed and flossed your teeth before going to bed!

Move ahead two spaces!

You helped your little brother with his homework!

Move ahead two spaces!

You kept your room clean all week!

Move ahead four spaces!

You got all of your church clothes ready on Saturday!

Move ahead two spaces!

You got ready for school on time!

Move ahead two spaces!

You did your chores without being asked!

Move ahead four spaces!

You did your chores without complaining!

Move ahead two spaces!

You put your coat and school books away after school!

Move ahead two spaces!

You went to bed on time and stayed there!

Move ahead two spaces!

You argued with your sister.

Move back two spaces.

You couldn't find your church shoes and made everyone late for church.

Move back four spaces.

You ate all of the cookies.

Move back two spaces.

You forgot to put your dirty clothes in the laundry and have nothing clean to wear.

Move back two spaces.

Be extra kind to someone. Trade places with the person in last place.

Whoops! You watched too much TV and forgot to do your chores.

Move back four spaces.

You complained about washing the dishes.

Move back two spaces.

You overslept and were late for school.

Move back two spaces.

You forgot to make your bed.

Move back two spaces.

You left your toys out.

Move back two spaces.

You didn't go to bed on time.

Move back two spaces.

You forgot to scrape your dinner plate.

Move back two spaces.

11

"Children of Light"

"Believe in the light, that ye may be the children of light."
John 12:36

OBJECT:

To help us understand that Jesus is the light of the world and that we can be children of light if we believe and follow him.

PREPARATION:

1. Copy the paper light bulbs on page 47 and the scripture cards on page 46. Cut them apart. Color the paper lightbulbs, if desired.
2. Gather tape, string, matches, a flashlight, a candle, scriptures, and a picture of Christ.
3. Prepare one room ahead of time by attaching the paper lightbulbs to various light sources throughout the room (ceiling light, lamp, candle, etc.) Turn off all the lights in the house except for the room where your family meets for family home evening. Display the picture of Christ in the room where it can be seen by all family members.

SUGGESTED SONG:

"Teach Me to Walk in the Light," *Children's Songbook*, page 177.

LESSON:

Pass the three scripture cards face down to your family members asking them not to look at what is written until you say so. Explain that written on the cards is important knowledge that will help us to understand the object of this lesson. Darken the room and ask the family members to read the cards. (Be sure to check the darkness of the room ahead of time making sure that the cards cannot be read!) Explain that knowledge is hard to gain without proper light. Turn on your flashlight, spotlighting the picture of Christ, and read D&C 11:11-14. Ask your family who is speaking in these verses. Who is the 'light which shineth in darkness'? To add to this discussion, have someone read card #1 (shining the flashlight for them as necessary). Now ask your family what they think "light" means in verse 11. To help come to an answer, have someone read card #2. Now ask your family to discuss verses 12 and 13, deciding on what a person will gain if they put their trust in the Lord. Have someone add to this discussion by reading card #3. Summarize the discussion by reminding the family that Christ is the light of the world. It is through Him that we receive joy and happiness. We should look to Him as an example for us to follow so that we can gain truth and knowledge and return to our Heavenly Father.

ACTIVITY:

With the lights in the room still off, shine the flashlight at the picture of Christ and read John 8:12. Explain to the family that they are going to follow the light through the darkness to discover greater truth and knowledge. Lead your family through the darkened house until you come to the previously prepared room. Read aloud D&C 50:24. Using the flashlight, search the room for various light sources. Start with the dimmest light source (the candle) and work your way to the brightest (ceiling light.) As you come to each light source, read and discuss what is written and then turn on (or light) the light source. Continue until all paper light bulbs have been found, read, and discussed, and the room is bright with light. In conclusion, read D&C 14:9. Explain to your family that light is always more powerful than darkness. Remind them that each time a light in the room was turned on, a little more darkness had to leave. The light of Christ cannot be hid. If we believe in Christ and keep his commandments, we will be known as children of light, securing our place in the Celestial kingdom and receiving a crown of glory (D&C 20:14).

Place the paper light bulbs in various places throughout the house to remind family members that they are all children of light.

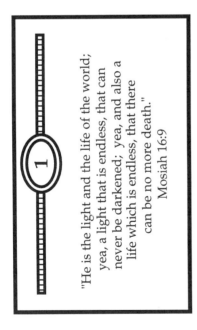

1

"He is the light and the life of the world; yea, a light that is endless, that can never be darkened; yea, and also a life which is endless, that there can be no more death."
Mosiah 16:9

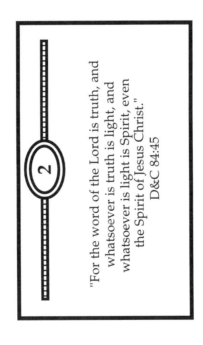

2

"For the word of the Lord is truth, and whatsoever is truth is light, and whatsoever is light is Spirit, even the Spirit of Jesus Christ."
D&C 84:45

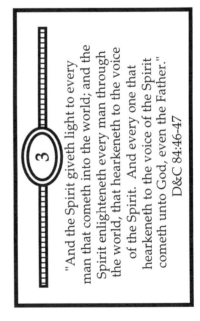

3

"And the Spirit giveth light to every man that cometh into the world; and the Spirit enlighteneth every man through the world, that hearkeneth to the voice of the Spirit. And every one that hearkeneth to the voice of the Spirit cometh unto God, even the Father."
D&C 84:46-47

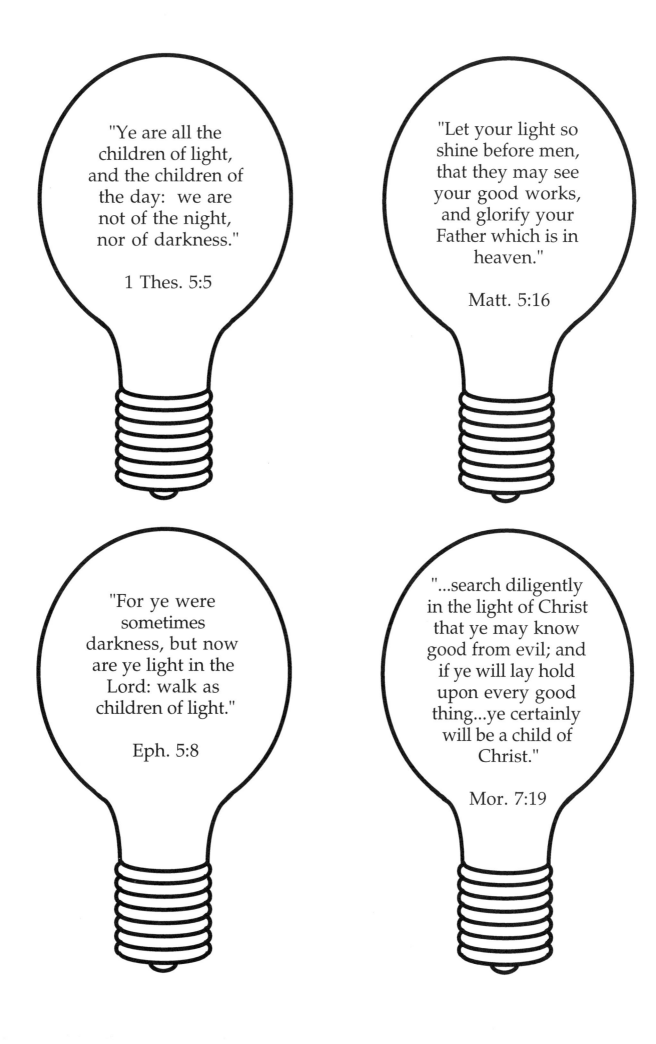

"Ye are all the children of light, and the children of the day: we are not of the night, nor of darkness."

1 Thes. 5:5

"Let your light so shine before men, that they may see your good works, and glorify your Father which is in heaven."

Matt. 5:16

"For ye were sometimes darkness, but now are ye light in the Lord: walk as children of light."

Eph. 5:8

"...search diligently in the light of Christ that ye may know good from evil; and if ye will lay hold upon every good thing...ye certainly will be a child of Christ."

Mor. 7:19

12

"Learn From Good Books"

"Seek ye out of the best books words of wisdom."
Doctrine and Covenants 109:7

OBJECT:

To help family members gain an appreciation for good books and church publications.

PREPARATION:

1. Make copies of the "Article Report" found on page 50.
2. Ask each family member to choose and read an article from one of the church publications, giving help to the younger members. Give each family member a copy of the "Article Report" to use in organizing their report.
3. Gather a variety of good books, magazines, scriptures, etc.

SUGGESTED SONG:

"Tell Me the Stories of Jesus," *Children's Songbook*, page 57.

LESSON:

Display the books, magazines, and scriptures for your family to see. Point to the display and explain that Heavenly Father has commanded us to learn from good books. Have someone read D&C 109:7. We should seek to learn from the best books things that would be pleasing to Heavenly Father. With the knowledge we gain, we should teach others to enlighten them also. In D&C 90:15, Heavenly Father commanded Joseph Smith to 'study and learn, and become acquainted with all good books, and with languages, tongues, and people.' Discuss with your family the blessings that would come to Joseph Smith (and others within his influence) if he were to follow this commandment. (Joseph would gain knowledge; knowledge that could be used to help organize the affairs of the church, and knowledge that could bring others to the gospel of Jesus Christ.) Read D&C 130:18-19. Explain to your family that the only thing we can bring with us to the next world is the knowledge that we have gained from this life through diligence and obedience. In verse 19 we learn that the more knowledge and intelligence we gain, the more advantage we will have in the world to come. The glory of God is intelligence (D&C 93:36) and God is more intelligent than all (Abraham 3:19). If we wish to become like God ourself, then we must diligently study and learn from good books (especially the scriptures) and prepare ourselves for the day when we will be crowned with glory and receive a complete understanding of everything.

ACTIVITY:

Take turns having family members report on their chosen article. If time allows, discuss the various sections of the church publications and how they can help us individually and as a family. Decide, as a family, a good time during the week for quiet reading of uplifting books and articles (possibly Sunday afternoon). If desired, devote a small amount of time during future family home evenings for an "Article Report." Alternate family members each week.

Handy Hint #2

Take time to pay weekly allowances during family home evening. Have tithing slips available to fill out, then tuck them away ready for Sunday.

Handy Hint #3

Try having your family home evenings in different settings. For instance, go to a park and have a lesson on God's creations. Or, set up a tent in the backyard and give a lesson on Lehi and his family in the wilderness. Have a lesson on genealogy at Grandma and Grandpa's house. Be creative!

Article Report

Title: _____

Author: _____

Where is the article found? _____

Why did you choose the article? _____

_____

Briefly describe the article: _____

_____

_____

_____

What did you learn from the article? _____

_____

_____

_____

Do you think others would like the article? Why? _____

_____

_____

Do you think others should read the article? Why? _____

_____

_____

13

"The Sabbath Day"

"Remember the sabbath day, to keep it holy."
Exodus 20:8

OBJECT:

To help family members learn what they can do to keep the Sabbath day holy.

PREPARATION:

1. Make the poster following the instructions given on page 53. Set the rectangles found on page 53 aside to be used during the lesson.
2. Write the following scriptures on paper and cut into individual strips:

    D&C 59:9   John 5:39
    D&C 19:38   Mosiah 2:17
    Mosiah 18:21 D&C 59:10
    D&C 25:12   Isaiah 54:13
    D&C 52:40   D&C 59:13

3. Gather two pieces of paper and a pen or pencil.

SUGGESTED SONG:

"Remember the Sabbath Day," *Children's Songbook*, page 155.

LESSON:

Begin by writing the days of the week, in order, on a piece of paper. Ask family members which day of the week is their favorite and why. Now ask them which one of the days is a special, sacred day. Circle Sunday. Ask your family if they know why Sunday is a sacred day. To help answer the question, have someone read Genesis 2:2-3. Heavenly Father labored for six days creating all things, both in heaven and earth. On the seventh day He rested. He sanctified (made holy) the seventh day and commanded all people to observe the Sabbath and keep it holy. Have someone read Exodus 20:8. Not only were the people in biblical days commanded to keep the Sabbath day holy, but the Nephites were commanded (Mosiah 18:23), and we, in modern times, are commanded to observe the Sabbath day (D&C 68:29). Heavenly Father will bless us if we obey this commandment (Isaiah 58:13-14, D&C 59:15-19).

ACTIVITY:

How can we keep the Sabbath day holy? The scriptures tell us many things that we can do to honor the Sabbath. Place the rectangles randomly on the floor or on a table. Place the strips of scriptures randomly by the rectangles. The object is to match the right scripture to the right rectangle. Have the family members choose a scripture, locate and read it, then decide which rectangle to pair it with. After the matches have been made, explain to your family that although the Sabbath is a day of rest, it is not a day to be lazy. It should be spent in worship and service to Heavenly Father. He has given us this day to replenish our bodies and spirits with physical and spiritual strength. To explain this point further, ask your family what would happen to the family car if it was driven continually without stopping for gas or regular maintenance. Eventually the car would run out of gas or break down. Without gas, or the needed repairs, the car would be useless. Our bodies and spirits are the same way. Without fuel and maintenance, provided through proper Sabbath day worship, our bodies and spirits would run down and become useless. We should be thankful to Heavenly Father for this wonderful commandment. Read Psalms 118:24 to your family.

Using another piece of paper, have your family make a list of things they usually do on the Sabbath. Review the list and decide, as a family, which activities are appropriate and which ones are not. A good way to decide if an activity is appropriate for the Sabbath is to ask, "Is this activity pleasing to Heavenly Father; does it show love and respect for him?" Show your family the poster you made prior to family home evening and demonstrate how it will help remind family members of appropriate Sabbath day activities. Encourage family members to show their love for Heavenly Father by observing the Sabbath.

HELPFUL HINT:

One way to help keep the Sabbath day holy is to prepare everything the day before on Saturday. By preparing ahead of time, we can eliminate the frantic search under the couch cushions for the missing shoe, sock, hair barrette, etc. Although, searching under the couch cushions usually rewards us with many lost items (so that's where the remote control was!) it usually makes everyone stressed and late for church. By preparing beforehand, time (and sanity) will be saved. It can also allow us extra time in the morning to deal with the last minute problems. (You know which ones I'm talking about: messy diapers, baby spit-up on your "dry-clean only" dress, the phone call reminding your child of the talk they forgot to tell you about!) Use the "Saturday Check List" on page 56 to help organize your Sunday mornings. After all, "If ye are prepared, ye shall not fear." D&C 38:30.

TO MAKE POSTER:

Copy this page onto card stock. Cut apart rectangles and color, if desired. Copy pages 54 and 55 onto card stock. Cut along thick, outside lines. Trim off the bottom edge of page 54 as indicated by the dashed line. Glue this edge to the top of page 55, matching all vertical lines and keeping the rectangle that is formed the same size as the rest of the rectangles. You should have ten rectangles in all. Color the poster, if desired. Display the poster in a prominant place along with the rectangles on this page. On Sunday, add the appropriate rectangles to the poster as each activity mentioned is accomplished. Encourage family members to keep the Sabbath day holy to show love and respect for Heavenly Father.

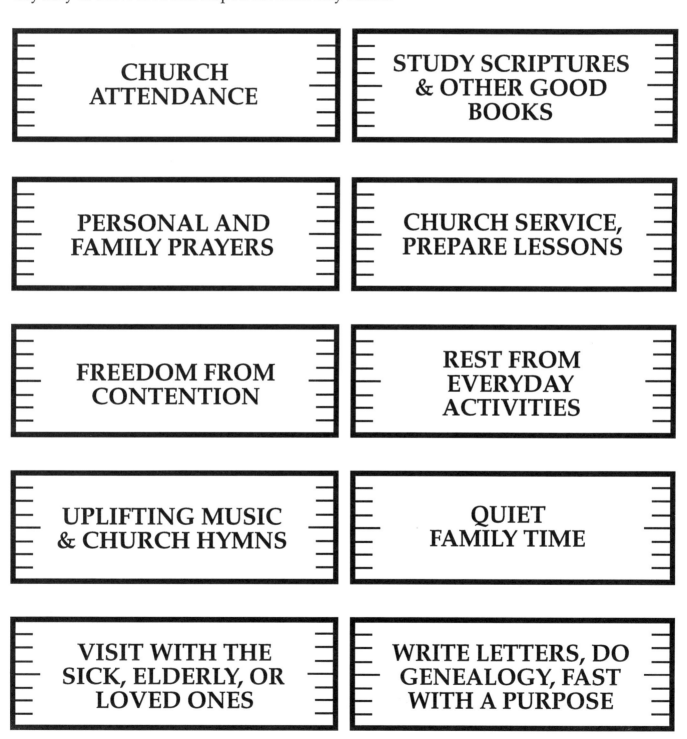

CHURCH ATTENDANCE

STUDY SCRIPTURES & OTHER GOOD BOOKS

PERSONAL AND FAMILY PRAYERS

CHURCH SERVICE, PREPARE LESSONS

FREEDOM FROM CONTENTION

REST FROM EVERYDAY ACTIVITIES

UPLIFTING MUSIC & CHURCH HYMNS

QUIET FAMILY TIME

VISIT WITH THE SICK, ELDERLY, OR LOVED ONES

WRITE LETTERS, DO GENEALOGY, FAST WITH A PURPOSE

"The observance of the Sabbath is an indication of the measure of our love for our Heavenly Father."

Spencer W. Kimball

How do we measure?

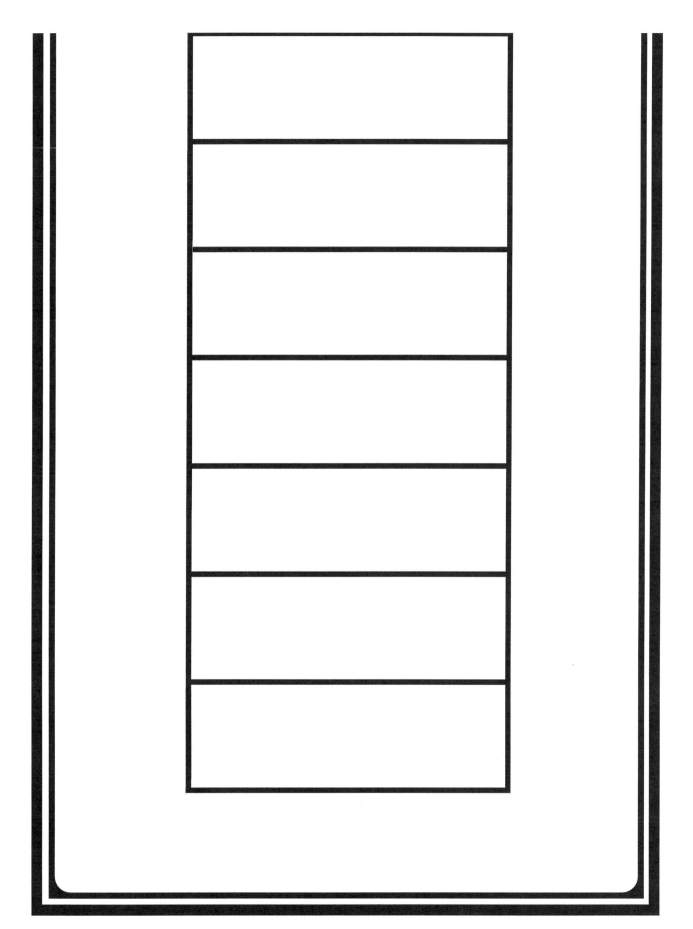

Saturday Check List

"Organize yourselves; prepare every needful thing."
D&C 88:119

- ☐ **Sunday Clothes** (cleaned and ironed)
- ☐ **Shoes and Socks**
- ☐ **Coats, if needed**
- ☐ **Scriptures**
- ☐ **Talks Prepared**
- ☐ **Food** (planned or prepared)
- ☐ **Lessons Prepared**
- ☐ **Diaper Bag Packed**
- ☐ **Tithing Slips Ready**
- ☐ **Little Ones Bathed**
- ☐ **House Clean and Tidy**

Hats Off to Family Home Evening!

Copy the hats on this page and the bears on page 58 (one bear and hat for each family member). Color and cut apart. Write the names of the family members on the bows and the family home evening responsibilities on the hats. Glue the bears, in a row, onto a piece of poster board following the example below. Draw a horizontal line at the feet of the bears as shown. Write the words "Hats off to family home evening!" at the bottom of the poster. Laminate the poster and hats. Use tape or "fun-tack" to attach and rotate hats each week.

Hat's Off To Family Home Evening!

Family Home Evening
Keeps Us Hanging Together!

Copy the clothing and two wooden posts on page 60 (one piece of clothing for each family member). Color and cut apart. Purchase miniature clothespins and use a permanent marker to label each clothespin with a family member's name. Write the family home evening responsibilities on the clothing. Glue the wooden posts onto poster board as shown below, allowing enough space for the clothing to hang in-between them. Write the words "Family home evening keeps us hanging together!" at the bottom of the poster. If desired, laminate the poster and clothing at this time. After laminating, poke a small hole at the top, inside edge of each post. Thread string through the holes from one post to the other allowing the string to sag slightly. Tape the string in place on the back side of the poster. Use the clothespins to hang the clothing on the line, rotating each week.

Family Home Evening Keeps Us Hanging Together!

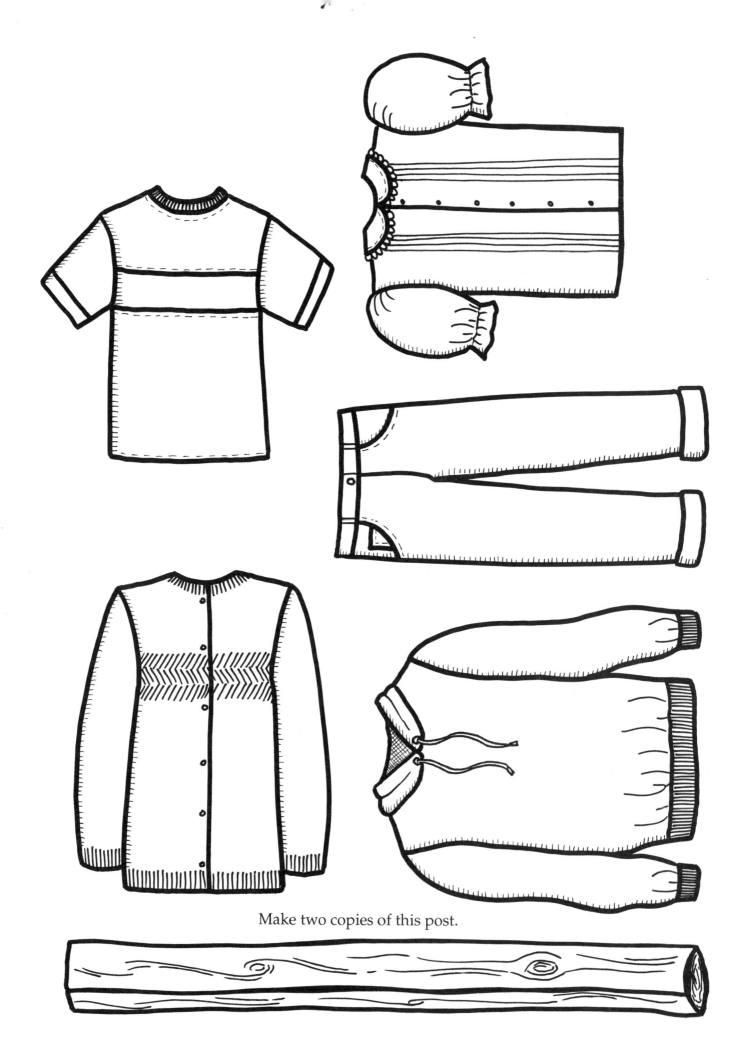

Make two copies of this post.